T0002338

A Mother's Love

A Book of Quotations

ixia
PRESS

Garden City, New York

Bibliographical Note

This Ixia Press edition, first published in 2022, is an updated, revised edition of *Mother: A Book of Quotations*, edited by Herb Galewitz, originally published by Dover Publications in 2002.

All images are courtesy of Getty Images.

Library of Congress Cataloging-in-Publication Data

Title: A mother's love : a book of quotations.
Description: Garden City, New York : Ixia Press, [2022] | "This Ixia Press edition, first published in 2022, is an updated, revised edition of Mother: A Book of Quotations, edited by Herb Galewitz, originally published by Dover Publications in 2002." | Summary: "This beautifully illustrated hardcover edition is filled with hundreds of quotations, sayings, and observations expressing gratitude and admiration for a mother's love. From the Roman poet Virgil to Michelle Obama, this delightful and entertaining collection speaks to the joys and rewards of motherhood through the wise and witty words of writers, state leaders, celebrities, and historical figures. A charming gift for birthdays, Mother's Day, or any other time of the year, this book is wonderful for browsing as a handy reference"—Provided by publisher.
Identifiers: LCCN 2021047878 | ISBN 9780486849591 (hardcover)
Subjects: LCSH: Mothers—Quotations. | Motherhood—Quotations, maxims, etc. | LCGFT: Quotations.
Classification: LCC PN6084.M6 M672 2022 | DDC 306.874/3—dc23/eng/20211103
LC record available at https://lccn.loc.gov/2021047878

IXIA PRESS
An imprint of Dover Publications

Manufactured in the United States of America
84959701   2022
www.doverpublications.com/ixiapress

The mother-child relationship is paradoxical and, in a sense, tragic. It requires the most intense love on the mother's side, yet this very love must help the child to grow away from the mother, and to become fully independent.

—Erich Fromm

To the best of her ability, a mother guides a child through infancy, childhood, and adolescence, providing him or her with unconditional love and support. While a mother may not be perfect, she generously offers understanding as she nurtures the confidence and independence that a child needs to survive. The special bond that exists between mother and child is a fluid one, resilient enough to withstand many inevitable changes. With patience, love, and a little luck, a mother takes great pride in the adult her child becomes and experiences the joy of watching this precious relationship develop into one of mutual respect, admiration, and affection.

This book is a loving appreciation of the countless things mothers do to help a child reach physical, emotional, and spiritual maturity. From the sweet and sentimental to the critical and analytical, the quotations in this book are a testament to the often complicated emotions that one feels toward mothers. Included in this thoughtful collection are proverbs and traditional sayings from around the world and insightful comments about motherhood in American society. The quotations are arranged alphabetically by author.

DID YOU EVER HEAR OF A GREAT AND GOOD MAN WHO HAD NOT A GOOD MOTHER?

—John Adams

Where there is a mother in the house, matters speed well.

—Amos Bronson Alcott

What *do* girls do who haven't any mothers to help them through their troubles?

—Louisa May Alcott

To describe my mother would be to write about a hurricane in its perfect power.

—Maya Angelou

When it comes to love, Mom's the word.

—*Anonymous*

Mothers are more devoted to their children than fathers . . . they suffer more in giving them birth and are more certain that they are their own.

—*Aristotle*

What tigress is there that does not purr over her young ones and fawn upon them in tenderness?

— *St. Augustine*

The joys of parents are secret,
and so are their griefs and fears.

—Francis Bacon

Instant availability without continuous presence is probably the best role a mother can play.

—LOTTE BAILYN

The heart of a mother is a deep abyss at the bottom of which you will always find forgiveness.

—HONORÉ DE BALZAC

For when you looked into my mother's eyes you knew, as if
He had told you, why God sent her into the world—it was
to open the minds of all who looked to beautiful thoughts.

—J. M. Barrie

My favorite thing about being a mom is just what a better person it makes you on a daily basis.

—*Drew Barrymore*

My wife is the kind of girl who'll not go anywhere without her mother, and her mother will go anywhere.

—*John Barrymore*

The future of society is in the hands of the mothers. If the world was lost through woman, she alone can save it.

—Louis de Beaufort

When God thought of mother, He must have laughed with satisfaction, and framed it quickly—so rich, so deep, so divine, so full of soul, power, and beauty, was the conception.

—Henry Ward Beecher

Her children arise up and call her blessed.

—The Bible

A smart mother makes often a better diagnosis than a poor doctor.

—AUGUST BIER

My mother groan'd! my father wept,
Into the dangerous world I leapt;
Helpless, naked, piping loud,
Like a fiend hid in a cloud.

—WILLIAM BLAKE

I take a very practical view of raising children. I put a sign in each of their rooms: "Checkout Time is 18 years."

—ERMA BOMBECK

I have reached the age when a woman begins to perceive that she is growing into the person she least plans to resemble: her mother.

—*Anita Brookner*

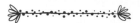

The sweetest sounds to mortals given
Are heard in Mother, Home, and Heaven.

—*William Goldsmith Brown*

What art can a woman be good at? Oh, vain!

What art *is* she good at, but hurting her breast

With the milk-teeth of babes, and a smile at the pain?

—Elizabeth Barrett Browning

Under Providence, I attribute any little distinction which I may have acquired in the world to the blessing which He conferred upon me in granting me such a mother.

—JAMES BUCHANAN

Some are kissing mothers and some are scolding mothers, but it is love just the same, and most mothers kiss and scold together.

—PEARL S. BUCK

Lo! at the couch where infant beauty sleeps,
Her silent watch the mournful mother keeps:
She, while the lovely babe unconscious lies,
Smiles on her slumbering child with pensive eyes.

—Thomas Campbell

Give me the life of the boy whose mother is nurse,
seamstress, washerwoman, cook, teacher, angel, and saint,
all in one, and whose father is guide, exemplar, and friend.
No servants to come between. These are the boys who are
born to the best fortune.

—Andrew Carnegie

How could Jimmy ever criticize me? I'm his mama.
—*Lillian Carter*

A mother's love for her child is like nothing else in the world. It knows no law, no pity. It dares all things and crushes down remorselessly all that stands in its path.

—*Agatha Christie*

A man may compass important enterprises, he may become famous, he may . . . deserve a measure of popular approval, but he is not right at heart, and can never be truly great, if he forgets his mother.

—*Grover Cleveland*

Mother of God! no lady thou.
Common woman of common earth!
—*Mary Elizabeth Coleridge*

So for the Mother's sake the Child was dear,
And dearer was the Mother for the Child.
—*Samuel Taylor Coleridge*

Those love-children always suffer because their mothers have crushed them under their stays trying to hide them, more's the pity. Yet after all, a lovely unrepentant creature, big with child, is not such an outrageous sight.

—*Colette*

There can be no proper observation of a birthday which forgets the mother.

—CALVIN COOLIDGE

Hundreds of dewdrops to greet the dawn;
Hundreds of lambs in the purple clover;
Hundreds of butterflies on the lawn;
But only one mother the wide world over.

—GEORGE COOPER

A rich child often sits in a poor mother's lap.

—DANISH PROVERB

Any suburban mother can state her role . . . it is to deliver children —
obstetrically once and by car forever after.

—Peter De Vries

A mother's arms are more comforting than anyone else's.

—Princess Diana

I think it must be somewhere written that the virtues of the mothers shall,
occasionally, be visited on their children, as well as the sins of the fathers.

—Charles Dickens

I never had a mother.
I suppose a mother is one
to whom you hurry
when you are troubled.

—*Emily Dickinson*

I think we're seeing in working mothers a change from "Thank God it's Friday" to "Thank God it's Monday." If any working mother has not experienced that feeling, her children are not adolescent.

—Ann Diehl

Cleaning your house while your kids are still growing is like shoveling the walk before it stops snowing.

—Phyllis Diller

I want a girl just like the girl that married dear old dad.

—William Dillon

No mother more indulgent but the true.
—John Dryden

What a price we pay for the glory of motherhood.
—Isadora Duncan

I believe that always, or almost always, in all childhoods and in all the lives that follow them, the mother represents madness. Our mothers always remain the strangest, craziest people we've ever met.

—Marguerite Duras

My mother was the making of me.
—Thomas Alva Edison

Take motherhood: nobody ever thought of putting it on a moral pedestal until some brash feminists pointed out, about a century ago, that the pay is lousy and the career ladder nonexistent.

—*Barbara Ehrenreich*

My life began with waking up and loving my mother's face.

—*George Eliot*

There was never a child so lovely but his mother was glad to get him asleep.

—*Ralph Waldo Emerson*

He that would the daughter win,
Must with the mother first begin.

—*English proverb*

For a short while, our mothers' bodies are the boundaries and
personal geography which are all that we know of the world. . . .
Once we no longer live beneath our mother's heart, it is the earth
with which we form the same dependent relationship.

—*Louise Erdrich*

It is safer in a mother's lap than in a lord's bed.

—*Estonian proverb*

I warned my son against taking home the foal of a bad mother.

—*Euripides*

If a writer has to rob his mother, he will not hesitate; the *Ode on a Grecian Urn* is worth any number of old ladies.

—*William Faulkner*

Mother Knows Best
—*Edna Ferber*

Being a mom has made me so tired. And so happy.

—Tina Fey

A mother is not a person to lean on but a person to make leaning unnecessary.

—DOROTHY CANFIELD FISHER

A friend can't take a mother's place. I need my mother as an example which I can follow. I want to be able to respect her.

—ANNE FRANK

First, *every* woman, I don't care who she is, prefers her son to her husband. . . . And why shouldn't she prefer someone who is so much like herself, who represents nine months of special concern and love and intense physical closeness—someone whom she actually created?

—Ian Frazier

The truth is that it is not the sins of the fathers that descend unto the third generation, but the sorrows of the mothers.

—Marilyn French

A man who has been the indisputable favorite of his mother keeps for life the feeling of conqueror, that confidence of success which often induces real success.

—Sigmund Freud

Strangely, many mothers who loved their daughters—and mine was one—did not want their daughters to grow up like them either. They knew we needed something more.

—Betty Friedan

Mother is food; she is love; she is warmth; she is earth. To be loved by her means to be alive, to be rooted, to be at home.

—Erich Fromm

A mother takes twenty years to make a man of her boy, and another woman makes a fool of him in twenty minutes.

—Robert Frost

It's not easy being a mother. If it were easy, fathers would do it.

—The Golden Girls

There is no shower for a woman when she completes the trimester of her life spent as a full-time mother. There is no midwife to help that woman deliver a healthy adult.

—Ellen Goodman

Lullaby, lullaby, thy mother is coming back
From the laurels by the river,
From the sweet banks she will bring thee flowers;
All sorts of flowers, roses, and scented pinks.

— Greek lullaby

Love is a roller coaster. Motherhood is a whole amusement park.

—Cathy Guisewite

A woman has two smiles that an angel might envy, the smile that accepts a lover before words are uttered, and the smile that lights on the first born babe, and assures it of a mother's love.

—Thomas Chandler Haliburton

You shall not take him, I care nothing for honour. I care only for the child that my womb has held, that my pain has brought forth, that my breasts have nourished. I care nothing for your wars. He was born of love; shall the blossom of love be destroyed by your hatreds?

—RADCLYFFE HALL

I find, by close observation, that the mothers are the levers which move in education. The men talk about it . . . but the women work most for it.

—FRANCES WATKINS HARPER

My mother was and will always remain my greatest hero.

— *Kamala Harris*

The commonest fallacy among women is that simply having children makes one a mother—which is as absurd as believing that having a piano makes one a musician.

—SYDNEY J. HARRIS

Everybody knows that a good mother gives her children a feeling of trust and stability. She is their earth. . . . Only to touch her skirt or her collar or her sleeve makes a troubled child feel better.

—KATHARINE BUTLER HATHAWAY

The successful mother sets her children free and becomes more free herself in the process.

—ROBERT J. HAVIGHURST

Before you were conceived I wanted you

Before you were born I loved you

Before you were here an hour I would die for you

This is the miracle of life.

—Maureen Hawkins

What is home without a mother?

—Alice Hawthorne

My mother was dead for five years before I knew that I had loved her very much.

—*Lillian Hellman*

The toughest part of motherhood is the inner worrying and not showing it.

—*Audrey Hepburn*

Other people's babies—
That's my life!
Mother to dozens,
And nobody's wife.
　　　　　　—*A. P. Herbert*

He that wipes the child's nose, kisseth the mother's cheek.
　　　　　　—*George Herbert*

The most important thing a father can do for his children is to love their mother.

—*Theodore Hesburgh*

Youth fades; love droops; the leaves of friendship fall:
A mother's secret hope outlives them all.

—*Oliver Wendell Holmes*

Thus she spoke, and I longed to embrace my dead mother's ghost. Thrice I tried to clasp her image, and thrice it slipped through my hands, like a shadow, like a dream.

—*Homer*

A man never sees all that his mother has been to him till it's too late to let her know that he sees it.

—*William Dean Howells*

The florists are everywhere the most ardent of matriolaters.

—*Aldous Huxley*

A man loves his sweetheart the most, his wife the best, but his mother the longest.

—*Irish proverb*

A mother is the truest friend we have, when trials, heavy and sudden fall upon us; when adversity takes the place of prosperity; when friends who rejoice with us in our sunshine, desert us when troubles thicken around us, still will she cling to us, and endeavor by her kind precepts and counsels to dissipate the clouds of darkness, and cause peace to return to our hearts.

— *Washington Irving*

This is a child who is always crying.
Be quiet, my soul, for mother is coming back.
She will bring thee nice milk,
And then put thee in the crib to hushaby.

—ITALIAN LULLABY

Motherhood is priced
Of God, at price no man may dare
To lessen or misunderstand.

—HELEN HUNT JACKSON

A mother never realizes that her children are no longer children.

—HOLBROOK JACKSON

God could not be everywhere and therefore
He made mothers.

—*Jewish saying*

In general, those parents have the most reverence
who most deserve it.

—*Samuel Johnson*

Now, as always, the most automated appliance
in a household is the mother.

—*Beverly Jones*

A mother is a person who, seeing there are only four pieces of pie for five people, promptly announces she never did care for pie.

—Tenneva Jordan

Whatever else is unsure in this stinking dunghill of a world a mother's love is not.

—James Joyce

Creative work arises from unconscious depths— we might truly say from the realm of the Mothers.

—Carl Jung

Motherhood . . . . Nothing else ever will make you as happy or as sad, as proud or as tired.

—*Marguerite Kelly and Elia Parsons*

Mothers all want their sons to grow up to be president, but they don't want them to become politicians in the process.

—John F. Kennedy

I looked upon child rearing . . . as a profession that was fully as interesting and challenging as any honorable profession in the world and one that demanded the best that I could bring to it.

— Rose Kennedy

Sometimes the strength of motherhood is greater than natural laws.
—BARBARA KINGSOLVER

If I were damned of body and soul,
I know whose prayers would make me whole,
Mother o' mine, O mother o' mine!
—RUDYARD KIPLING

Mother's love grows by giving.
—CHARLES LAMB

She seems to have had the ability to stand firmly on the rock of her past while living completely and unregretfully in the present.

—MADELEINE L'ENGLE

All that I am, or hope to be, I owe to my angel mother.

—ABRAHAM LINCOLN

By and large, mothers and housewives are the only workers who do not have regular time off. They are the great vacationless class.

—ANNE MORROW LINDBERGH

Of course, everybody knows that the greatest thing about Motherhood is the "Sacrifices," but it is quite a shock to find out that they begin so far ahead of time.

–Anita Loos

When you are a mother, you are never really alone in your thoughts. You are connected to your child and to all those who touch your lives. A mother always has to think twice, once for herself and once for her child.

–Sophia Loren

The many make the household,
But only one the home.

–James Russell Lowell

You may have friends, fond, dear, kind friends; but never will you have again the inexpressible love and gentleness lavished upon you which none but a mother bestows.
—*Thomas Babington Macaulay*

I would weave you a song, my mother . . .
Yours the tender hand upon my breast;
Yours the voice sounding ever in my ears.
—*Madeline Mason-Manheim*

Few misfortunes can befall a boy which bring worse consequences than to have a really affectionate mother.
—*W. Somerset Maugham*

Your love for your mother is something
that you never completely comprehend
until you are separated by the miles from
her warmth and her wonder.

—Collin McCarty

A mother's hardest to forgive.
Life is the fruit she longs to hand to you,
Ripe on a plate. And while you live
Relentlessly she understands you.

—PHYLLIS MCGINLEY

One of the oldest human needs is having someone to
wonder where you are when you don't come home at night.

—MARGARET MEAD

It is only in our advanced and synthetic civilization that
mothers no longer sing to the babies they are carrying.

—YEHUDI MENUHIN

This heart, my own dear mother, bends,
With love's true instinct, back to thee!

—Thomas Moore

Every beetle is a gazelle in the eyes of its mother.

—Moorish proverb

Heaven is at the feet of mothers.

—Muslim proverb

Children aren't happy with nothing to ignore,
And that's what parents were created for.

—Ogden Nash

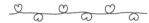

One moment makes a father, but a mother
Is made by endless moments, load on load.

—John G. Neihardt

She did not understand how her father could have reached
such age and such eminence without learning that all mothers
are as infallible as any pope and more righteous than any saint.

—Frances Newman

I don't think that all good mothers have to bake and sew and make beds and wear percale bungalow aprons. Some of the finest never go into their kitchens at all; some of the most devoted are also some of the richest.

—KATHLEEN NORRIS

Clearly, society has a tremendous stake in insisting on
a woman's natural fitness for the career of mother:
the alternatives are all too expensive.

—ANN OAKLEY

Being a mother has been a masterclass in letting go.
Try as we might, there's only so much we can control.

—MICHELLE OBAMA

I think in a lot of ways unconditional love is a myth.
My mom's the only reason I know it's a real thing.

—CONOR OBERST

If you bungle raising your children, I don't think whatever else you do well matters very much.

—*Jacqueline Kennedy Onassis*

With more fortitude does a mother long for one out of many, than she who weeping cries, "Thou wast my only one."

—*Ovid*

Every man must define his identity against his mother. If he does not, he just falls back into her and is swallowed up.

—*Camille Paglia*

One scream of fear from a mother may resound through the whole life of her daughter.

—*Jean Paul*

Every mother is like Moses. She does not enter the promised land. She prepares a world she will not see.

—*Pope Paul VI*

THE BEST PLACE TO CRY
IS ON A MOTHER'S ARMS.

–Jodi Picoult

One is the race of men, another is the race of gods,
but from one mother we both draw our breath.

—Pindar

The angels, whispering to one another,
Can find, among their burning terms of love,
None so devotional as that of "Mother."

—Edgar Allan Poe

The greatest love is a mother's; then comes a dog's;
then comes a sweetheart's.

—Polish proverb

Diligent mother, idle daughter.
—*Portuguese proverb*

Motherhood . . . is still the biggest gamble in the world. It is the glorious life force. It's huge and scary—it's an act of infinite optimism.
—*Gilda Radner*

Romance fails us and so do friendships, but the relationship of mother and child remains indelible and indestructible—the strongest bond on earth.
—*Theodor Reik*

Oh, to be only half as wonderful as my child thought I was when he was small, and only half as stupid as my teenager now thinks I am.

—*Rebecca Richards*

No joy in nature is so sublimely affecting as the joy of a mother at the good fortune of her child.

—*Jean Paul Richter*

Mothers are the only race of people that speak the same tongue. A mother in Manchuria could converse with a mother in Nebraska and never miss a word.

—*Will Rogers*

I think, at a child's birth, if a mother could ask a fairy godmother to endow it with the most useful gift, that gift would be curiosity.

—*Eleanor Roosevelt*

The mother is the one supreme asset of national life; she is more important by far than the successful statesman, or business man, or artist, or scientist.

—*Theodore Roosevelt*

We are born of love. Love is our mother.

—*Rumi*

A mother loves her children even when
they least deserve to be loved.

—*Kate Samperi*

When motherhood becomes the fruit of a deep yearning, not the result of ignorance or accident, its children will become the foundation of a new race.

—MARGARET SANGER

The ideal mother, like the ideal marriage, is a fiction.

—MILTON R. SAPIRSTEIN

Children reinvent your world for you.

—SUSAN SARANDON

My mother is everywhere . . .
In the perfume of a rose,
The eyes of a tiger,
The pages of a book,
The food we partake,
The whistling wind of the desert,
The blazing gems of sunset,
The crystal light of full moon,
The opal veils of sunrise.

—Grace Seton-Thompson

Motherhood has relaxed me in many ways. You learn to deal with crisis.
I've become a juggler, I suppose. It's all a big circus, and nobody who
knows me believes I can manage, but sometimes I do.

—Jane Seymour

We should honor mothering for what it is: the hardest job in the world.
It's one that deserves our respect, our devotion, and our love every day.

—Maria Shriver

Do not join encounter groups. If you enjoy being
made to feel inadequate, call your mother.

—Liz Smith

Sons are the anchors of a mother's life.
—SOPHOCLES

An ounce of mother is worth a pound of clergy.
—SPANISH PROVERB

I really learned it all from mothers.
—BENJAMIN SPOCK

Though motherhood is the most important of all the professions—requiring more knowledge than any other department in human affairs—there was no attention given to preparation for this office.

—*Elizabeth Cady Stanton*

It's clear that most American children suffer too much mother and too little father.

—*Gloria Steinem*

Making the decision to have a child—it's momentous. It is to decide forever to have your heart go walking around outside your body.

—*Elizabeth Stone*

MOTHERS ARE THE MOST INSTINCTIVE PHILOSOPHERS.

—*Harriet Beecher Stowe*

Motherhood has a very humanizing effect.
Everything else gets reduced to essentials.

—MERYL STREEP

Who ran to help me when I fell,
And would some pretty story tell,
Or kiss the place to make it well?

My mother.

—ANN TAYLOR

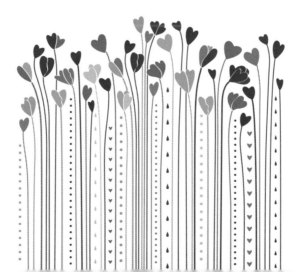

Happy he
With such a mother! Faith in womankind
Beats with his blood, and truth in all things high
Comes easy to him.

—Alfred, Lord Tennyson

My mother had a great deal of trouble with me,
but I think she enjoyed it.

—Mark Twain

If you want your children to turn out well, spend twice
as much time with them, and half as much money.

—Abigail Van Buren

I knew what I had to have before my soul would rest. I wanted to belong—to belong to my mother. And in return—I wanted my mother to belong to me.

—*Gloria Vanderbilt*

Begin, little boy, to recognize your mother with a smile.

—*Virgil*

My best creation is my children.

—*Diane von Furstenberg*

We have a beautiful
mother
Her green lap
immense
Her brown embrace
eternal
Her blue body
everything
we know.
   —ALICE WALKER

The hand that rocks the cradle
   Is the hand that rules the world.
            —WILLIAM ROSS WALLACE

All I am I owe to my mother. I attribute all my success in life to the moral, intellectual, and physical education I received from her.

—*George Washington*

I was not a classic mother. But my kids were never palmed off to boarding school. So, I didn't bake cookies. You can buy cookies, but you can't buy love.

—*Raquel Welch*

Ah, lucky girls who grow up in the shelter of a mother's love— a mother who knows how to contrive opportunities without conceding favours, how to take advantage of propinquity without allowing appetite to be dulled by habit!

—*Edith Wharton*

To her, the ideal woman, practical, spiritual, of all of earth,
life, love, to me the best.

—*Walt Whitman*

All women become like their mothers. That is their tragedy.
No man does. That's his.

—*Oscar Wilde*

My father got me strong and straight and slim,
    And I give thanks to him;
My mother bore me glad and sound and sweet,
    I kiss her feet.

—*Marguerite Wilkinson*

Biology is the least of what makes
someone a mother.

—Oprah Winfrey

━━━∽∾ᴇ ᴈ∾━━━

Mama was my greatest teacher, a teacher of compassion, love
and fearlessness. If love is sweet as a flower, then my mother
is that sweet flower of love.

—Stevie Wonder

━━━∽∾ᴇ ᴈ∾━━━

Years to a mother bring distress;
But do not make her love the less.

—William Wordsworth